For Mom (and in thanks to Jackie Chan), for keeping us entertained all those years —K.M.G.

For my parents and my childhood home, Hong Kong, for giving me many beautiful memories —A.C.

Text copyright © 2022 by Kristen Mai Giang
Jacket art and interior illustrations copyright © 2022 by Alina Chau

All rights reserved. Published in the United States by Crown Books for Young Readers,
an imprint of Random House Children's Books, a division of Penguin Random House LLC, New York.

Crown and the colophon are registered trademarks of Penguin Random House LLC.

Visit us on the Web! rhcbooks.com

Educators and librarians, for a variety of teaching tools, visit us at RHTeachersLibrarians.com

Library of Congress Cataloging-in-Publication Data is available upon request.
ISBN 978-0-593-12192-4 (hardcover) — ISBN 978-0-593-12193-1 (lib. bdg.) — ISBN 978-0-593-12194-8 (ebook)

The text of this book is set in 14-point BernhardGothicSCGOT.
The illustrations in this book were created using watercolor.
Book design by Monique Razzouk

MANUFACTURED IN CHINA
10 9 8 7 6 5 4 3 2 1
First Edition

THE RISE (AND FALLS) OF JACKIE CHAN

written by Kristen Mai Giang

illustrated by Alina Chau

Crown Books for Young Readers ♛ New York

Jackie and his father met every sunrise with kung fu.

POW! BAM! OW!

Ba Ba said kung fu taught discipline, focus.
Jackie was NOT disciplined.
He could focus on only one thing . . . his empty belly!
As soon as he could, he raced inside for breakfast.

Jackie lived at the ambassador's mansion in Hong Kong.
Ma Ma did the laundry. Ba Ba cooked.
They all slept in one bunk in one room.
Poor but happy.

Though Jackie did get into trouble sometimes.
When neighborhood bullies teased his friend, Jackie defended her with his fists.

POW! BAM! OW!

He joked around in school. Made funny faces. Faked falling over and over.

OW! OW! OW!

Jackie was NOT a star student. Teacher made him wear a sign: USELESS.
His parents despaired. What would become of him?

Ba Ba and Ma Ma had to move to Australia for work.
They needed more money. They couldn't live in one room forever.
His father decided to enroll Jackie in the China Drama Academy,
where poor, unwanted, or unruly children trained for Chinese opera.
Jackie would stay at the academy for the next ten years.

中國戲劇學院

出入平安

龍馬精神

The academy was a shock of hard work and discipline.
Students trained from five in the morning to midnight.
Acting, singing, martial arts. Flips, splits, somersaults.
They suffered injuries frequently and silently.

Disobedience earned the sting of Master's stick.
And Jackie was NOT always obedient.

THWACK!
THWACK!
THWACK!

Order was absolute, from oldest to youngest. As Littlest Brother, Jackie was lowest of the low. If Biggest Brother demanded his candy, Jackie handed it over.

Then the new Littlest Brother arrived. Shy and talented, he was an easy target. But Jackie was NOT a quiet bystander. He stood up for Littlest Brother.

POW! BAM! OW!

Months passed with long days of bruises and scrapes and narrow escapes.

Then Jackie saw what he'd been training for all that time.

A real Chinese opera.

CLANG! BANG! THWACK!

Painted faces. Swirling colors. Epic battles.

The audience roared.

Jackie's heart beat with the drums.

That could be *him*.

Jackie was NOT the best at anything—fighting, acting, acrobatics. But he worked with all his heart. And it paid off. Jackie was chosen as one of the Seven Little Fortunes—the academy's star performers. He traveled from stage to stage with Biggest Brother and Littlest Brother, who were chosen too. His unlikely new family.

One day after a performance, they tried to ride the bus for free.

Chased by the ticket taker, they raced to the upper level of the speeding double-decker.

And jumped out the window.

It was the first terrifying stunt of Jackie's life.

As Jackie grew up, audiences for Chinese opera dwindled.
The Hong Kong movie scene exploded with martial arts.
Stuntmen were suddenly in demand.

Nameless and faceless, they performed fights, falls, and flips.

The cameras never stopped when they got hurt.

With no money or education, Jackie risked his neck day after day.

POW! BAM! OW!

But at night, he watched movies.
From Hong Kong cinema to the Hollywood silver screen.
The fearless feats of comedian Buster Keaton.
The funny faces of actor Charlie Chaplin.
The flying feet of dancer Fred Astaire.

His heart beat with the music.

That could be *him*!

One day, a director demanded a deadly stunt.

"No wires!"

Jackie volunteered, desperate to stand out.

He fell off a balcony backward. Blindly counted the seconds.

Twisted in the air.

BAM!

And landed on his feet.

Jackie became a top stuntman.

But he was still nameless and faceless on screen.

The actors were handsome and perfect.

NOT rough-and-tumble boys like him.

Then Jackie met someone who changed everything.

李小龍

Bruce Lee blew up martial arts movies with his modern street-fighting style. For Jackie, he was a new kind of star. Someone real. Someone like him. Jackie did stunts in two of Bruce Lee's movies, *Fist of Fury* and *Enter the Dragon*.

When Bruce Lee passed away, studios scrambled to find a replacement.

Jackie got his big break starring in the Bruce Lee remake, *New Fist of Fury*.
But the movie flopped. His studio boss put him in movie after movie modeled after
Bruce Lee, the invincible.

FLOP. FLOP. FLOP.

Jackie still didn't fit the part everyone wanted him to play. He was NOT Bruce Lee.

To make himself feel better, Jackie joked around on set.

Made funny faces. Faked falling over and over.

Used silly props like brooms and toupees in fights as intricate as a dance.

DUCK. DODGE. JUMP. SLIDE.
DUCK. DODGE. JUMP. SLIDE.

Jackie developed his own style.

Buster Keaton with kung fu flair and a little Fred Astaire.

His studio boss hated it. He told Jackie to *just* be like Bruce Lee.

But by then, Jackie knew who he was NOT.

And who he was.

He went to another studio and finally got to be Jackie.

A boy who became a hero by being himself,

POW! BAM! OW!

made martial arts creative and fun,

SNAKE! EAGLE! CAT!

and did all his own stunts.

OW! OW! OW!

Snake in the Eagle's Shadow was a smash. The first-ever kung fu comedy. Jackie, the penniless Hong Kong kid, became a star.

蛇形刁手

Jackie would make more than 150 movies. But some things never changed. In his movies, he jumped from speeding double-deckers. Made funny faces. Faked falling over and over.

POW! BAM! OW!

He was always true to himself.

GLOSSARY OF CHINESE CHARACTERS

Cantonese and Mandarin pronunciations are provided for each entry.

成龍 **Sing Lung / Cheng Long** — Jackie Chan's Chinese name (page 3)

沒用 **mut yung / mei yong** — useless (page 10)

出入平安 **Cheut Yap Ping On / Chu Ru Ping An** — Peace and safety to all who enter and leave (page 11)

中國戲劇學院 **Jung Gwok Hei Kek Hok Yun / Zhong Guo Xi Ju Xue Yuan** — China Drama Academy (page 11)

龍馬精神 **Lung Ma Jing San / Long Ma Jing Shen** — May you have the strength and health of a dragon or horse (page 11)

武 **mou / wu** — martial arts (page 12)

李小龍 **Lei Siu Lung / Lee Xiao Long** — Bruce Lee's Chinese name (page 26)

蛇刑刁手 **Se Ying Dou Sau / She Xing Diao Shou** — *Snake in the Eagle's Shadow* (page 33)

AUTHOR'S NOTE

I recall watching Jackie Chan movies in the old San Gabriel Valley, California, theater that showed all-day double features from Hong Kong. There were no age restrictions. No matter the movie, Mom bought tickets for herself and all six kids. Fighting over spicy, sticky, fruit-flavored beef jerky, we gaped and laughed at Jackie's antics, then ran home and practiced kung fu on each other. I suspect my older siblings were inspired by *Drunken Master* when they disciplined us hapless younger ones. Jackie Chan wouldn't become famous in America until decades later, but to us he was a star we could relate to even from across the world.

Early Goodbyes

Jackie Chan's parents, Charles and Lee-Lee Chan, were so poor they almost sold Jackie to the doctor who delivered him. In the early 1950s, Hong Kong—a peninsula and group of islands off the coast of mainland China—was still under British rule and awash with immigrants escaping the Chinese Civil War. Not only was it difficult to find work, but many immigrant families, including Jackie's, had already lost loved ones. Separating from one's children and other family members was heartbreaking but not unusual. With Jackie's father moving to Australia to make more money, and Jackie not doing well in school and getting into trouble, his parents felt the academy was the best option. His mother stayed in Hong Kong working at the French ambassador's mansion for another two years, visiting Jackie weekly until she ultimately left too. Jackie called her "the best mom in the world."

Missed Education

Jackie Chan has often stated that one of his biggest regrets is his lack of education. He didn't do well in school at an early age, failing his first year before his parents pulled him out. Actual academics were not emphasized at the academy. Though he has clearly found success, he says, "You can't ever go back again. . . . I could have been the world's most famous doctor. Instead of the world's most famous patient."

School of Hard Knocks

Although he suffered greatly at the hands of Master Yu Jim-yuen of the China Drama Academy, Jackie later acknowledged him for being the father of Jackie Chan. His training, brutal as it was, unacceptable as it would be today, fueled Hong Kong martial arts movies for decades with dozens of highly trained students like Jackie, Biggest Brother (Sammo Hung), and Littlest Brother (Yuen Biao). Besides learning skills for Chinese opera, Jackie got early experience as a child actor in various movies like *Big and Little Wong Tin Bar* (1962). But it was his irrepressible spirit that made him a star. Master Yu has been quoted describing Jackie as "not the best, but the naughtiest, yes."

Lung Fu Mo Shi

Jackie has credited stunt work as his third school of training, after his early kung fu training with his father and the China Drama Academy. In this world of brave, brash stuntmen who risked their lives every day for low pay and little protection, Jackie found a new family. He embraced their spirit of *lung fu mo shi*, invoking the power and courage of dragon (*lung*) and tiger (*fu*) as the ultimate kung fu master. It was this philosophy of facing your fears, failing at a stunt, and then getting up to do it again that would eventually drive Jackie's world-class stunts.

Becoming "Jackie"

Jackie's road to stardom was long and difficult. Although he succeeded early on as a stuntman, stunt work could be elusive as the Hong Kong film industry suffered hardships. Jackie even left Hong Kong to live with his parents in Australia a couple of times when he couldn't find work. While in Australia, Jackie took odd jobs like dishwashing and construction work. It was his Australian construction boss Jack who named Jackie, telling the crew that his name was Jack too. Jackie was born Chan Kong-sang, meaning "born in Hong Kong," and he took the Chinese stage name Sing Lung, meaning "already a dragon," in 1976.

Jackie of All Trades

In addition to starring in more than one hundred movies and famously doing all his own stunts for years, Jackie wrote, directed, and produced many of his movies. If you listen carefully, you'll even hear Jackie singing during the credits (and soundtracks) of all of his Chinese movies.

Bibliography

Chan, Jackie, and Jeff Yang. *I Am Jackie Chan: My Life in Action.* New York: Ballantine, 1998.

Chan, Jackie, and Zhu Mo. *Never Grow Up.* New York: Gallery Books, 2018.

Gentry, Clyde, III. *Jackie Chan: Inside the Dragon.* Dallas: Taylor Trade Publishing, 1997.

Little, John R., and Curtis F. Wong. *Jackie Chan.* The Best of Inside Kung-Fu. Chicago: Contemporary Books, 1999.

Stone, Amy. *Jackie Chan.* Milwaukee: Gareth Stevens Publishing, 2007.

Witterstaetter, Renée. *Dying for Action: The Life and Films of Jackie Chan.* New York: Warner Books, 1997.